It's a WILDLIFE, Buddy!

Josh
the Anteater

Daniela De Luca

WORLD BOOK

World Book, Inc.
180 North LaSalle Street
Suite 900
Chicago, Illinois 60601
USA

For school and library sales, please phone
1-800-975-3250 (United States)
or 1-800-837-5365 (Canada).

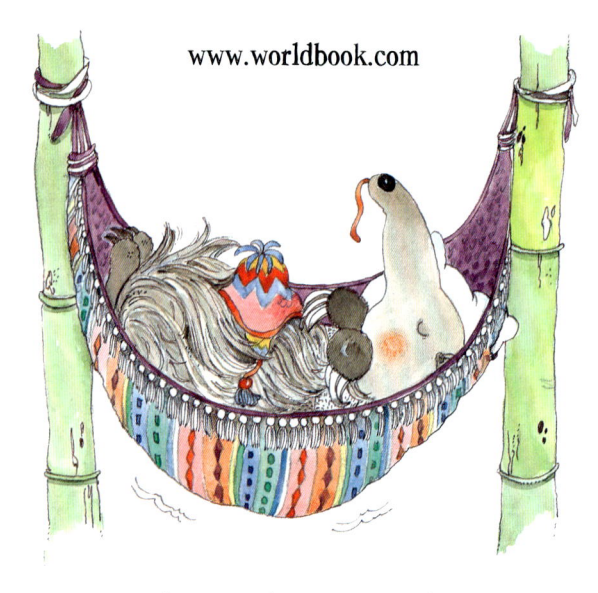

www.worldbook.com

LIBRARY OF CONGRESS
CATALOGING-IN-PUBLICATION DATA
HAS BEEN APPLIED FOR.

Copyright © 2017 by Nextquisite Ltd, London
Publishers: Anne McRae, Marco Nardi
www.nextquisite.com

All illustrations by Daniela De Luca
Texts: Daniela De Luca, Anne McRae, Neil Morris
Editing: Anne McRae, Vicky Egan, Neil Morris
Graphic Design: Marco Nardi
Layout: Marco Nardi, Rebecca Milner

All rights reserved. No part of this book may be reproduced in any form without the prior written permission of the copyright owner.

This edition edited and revised by World Book, Inc.
by permission of Nextquisite Ltd.

ISBN: 978-0-7166-3519-2 (set), 978-0-7166-3525-3 (Josh the Anteater)

Printed and bound in China
1st printing March 2017

VENEZUELA
COLOMBIA
GUYANA
SURINAME
FRENCH GUIANA
ECUADOR
BRAZIL
PERU
BOLIVIA
PARAGUAY
PACIFIC OCEAN
URUGUAY
CHILE
ARGENTINA
ATLANTIC OCEAN

It is a bright, sunny morning on the South American **grasslands**, and Josh and his mother are having breakfast.

WHAT DO ANTEATERS EAT?

Ants, of course! And **termites**. The ants and termites live in tall mounds that dot the grasslands. An anteater can eat up to 30,000 of these insects and their eggs in one day!

HOW LONG IS AN ANTEATER'S TONGUE?

It's up to 24 inches (60 cm) long! The anteater flicks it in and out of holes in the mound, and the ants stick to it.

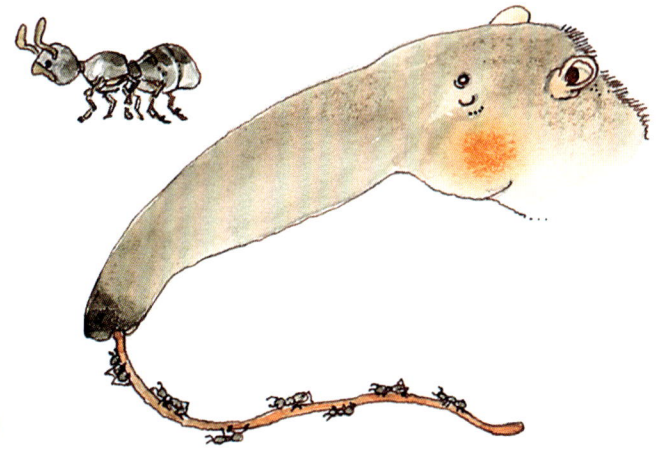

TODAY IS A SPECIAL DAY for Josh. His mother has promised to take him to the big market that is held far away in the Andes Mountains.

IT'S A LONG AND DANGEROUS JOURNEY from the grasslands up into the mountains. After a steep climb, Josh and his mother can see the market on the other side of a deep valley. They have to cross a wobbly rope bridge to get there.

HOW DOES AN ANTEATER CARRY HER CUB?

A mother anteater lets her cub ride piggyback. If the cub falls off, it makes a shrill sound to tell its mother! Anteater mothers carry their cubs this way for about one year.

THEY MAKE IT SAFELY ACROSS and find themselves in a noisy, colorful crowd. The air is full of the smell of freshly baked honey-and-ant cookies and the sweet sound of flute music. Josh asks his mother if she will buy him a flute.

THE NEXT DAY AT SCHOOL, Josh takes out his new flute and shows it to his friends. They all crowd around to listen as he gently blows into it through his nose. The only one missing is Josh's best friend Dillo the armadillo, who is out sick.

MICAELA SPIDER MONKEY

BIANCA VAMPIRE BAT

CARLITO CAPYBARA

JOSH

JUAN FELIPE PECCARY

TIMOTHY AND THOMAS TAPIR

CATHY COATI

EVERETT AND STELLA TOUCAN

PANGOLIN

WHO ARE THESE STRANGE CREATURES?
Like anteaters, the scaly pangolin and the donkey-eared, pig-nosed aardvark both eat ants and termites. But they live far away from anteaters. Pangolins live in Africa and Asia, and aardvarks live in Africa.

AARDVARK

MS. VIOLETA TAPIR

AUGUSTÍN AGOUTI

AFTER SCHOOL, Josh hurries off to visit his friend Dillo. The armadillos live on the pampas, or dry plains, just beyond the rain forest.

Josh says hello to Mother Armadillo and shows her his flute. Then he gives her a basket of goodies that his mother made for Dillo's large family.

WHY DO ANTEATERS SNIFF SO MUCH?
Anteaters can't see well, so they find things by using their noses. They sniff the ground to find their way about.

DILLO

DILLO IS IN BED, and he's not feeling well at all. Josh plays him a tune on his flute, but he isn't good at it yet and sometimes makes sounds that are noise rather than music! Dillo starts to giggle. Josh's music makes him feel much better.

13

WHAT IS A RAIN FOREST?

It is a warm, wet forest where giant trees tower above smaller trees, and it almost never stops raining! Millions of animals live there, from squawking birds and chattering monkeys to huge snakes and many different kinds of insects.

LATER, JOSH WAVES GOODBYE to the armadillos and heads off home through the rain forest.

WHY DO ANTEATERS WALK IN SUCH A CLUMSY WAY?

Anteaters can't put their front feet flat because their curved claws are too long. Instead, they walk on their outer knuckles, and this makes them move slowly.

Enrico Boa Constrictor

Federico and Walter Woolly Monkey

Angelo and Tina Peccary

Antonia and Sara Capybara

16

JOSH FEELS SCARED in the noisy rain forest. He sees lots of different animals in the trees and on the forest floor. He tries not to trip over the big tree roots and not to walk into the vines hanging down from the branches.

JOE THREE-TOED SLOTH

TERRY NEW WORLD PORCUPINE

JOSH

PEDRO AND PABLITO POISON DART FROG

TILLY AND TOT
TOUCAN

STEFANO SILKY
ANTEATER

HUMMER
AND BUZZ
HUMMINGBIRD

JILLY JAGUAR

ARNOLDO
AND
ARTURO
AGOUTI

18

Orazio Two-Toed Sloth

Filippo Macaw

Felipe Parrot

Barry Bat

Timo Southern Tamandua

Juan Turtle

SUDDENLY A GIANT **ANACONDA** slides out of the swampy water and surprises Josh. He runs off as fast as he can.

CAN ANTEATERS GO FAST?
Anteaters usually shuffle along, or move slowly, but they can move quickly when they are frightened.

THEN AN EAGLE swoops down with her sharp **talons** out. Josh only just escapes.

CAN ANTEATERS SWIM?
Yes, they are good swimmers. They often take a dip in South America's mighty Amazon River.

Josh is so frightened that he runs straight toward a big, roaring jaguar. It gives him such a fright that he falls over. Who can save him now?

23

24

THAT'S LUCKY! Looking up, Josh sees his mother waving her sharp claws at the big cat. Mother came to look for him, and he has never seen her look so **fierce**! She is certainly too scary for the jaguar.

WHAT DO ANTEATERS USE THEIR CLAWS FOR?

If threatened, an anteater will stand up and use its long, sharp claws to defend itself. It also uses them to tear open termite mounds and anthills.

DO ANTEATERS SLEEP MUCH?
Yes. Giant anteaters sleep at night, but they don't sleep deeply. Even a small noise will wake them. So they also take lots of naps during the day. They curl up under their long, bushy tails to keep warm.

ON THE WAY HOME, Josh is so tired that Mother Anteater has to carry him. He falls fast asleep and is soon dreaming of crispy fried ants, fresh from his mother's oven.

27

THREE-TOED SLOTH

TWO-TOED SLOTH

NINE-BANDED ARMADILLO

DID YOU KNOW?

Anteaters, sloths, and armadillos often share a habitat, the area where an animal naturally lives. As people use up more land and there is less habitat, it is hard for animals to find food and safe places to live.

GIANT ARMADILLO

PINK FAIRY ARMADILLO

SILKY ANTEATER

SOUTHERN TAMANDUA

(ANIMALS ARE NOT SHOWN TO SCALE.)

JOSH

HAIRY ARMADILLO

29

TOUCAN

THREE-TOED SLOTH

BOA CONSTRICTOR

SPECTACLED BEAR

Here is Josh with many of the animals he knows. They all live in Central or South America. How many of his friends do you recognize?

VAMPIRE BAT

CONDOR

PATAGONIAN HARE

TAPIR

CAPYBARA

PECCARY

Hummingbird

Tree porcupine

Tamandua

(Animals are not shown to scale.)

Vicuña

Llama

Spider monkey

Blue and yellow macaw

Josh

Chinchilla

Jaguar

Rhea

Pink fairy armadillo

Giant armadillo

Anaconda

Poison dart frog

Tortoise

Glossary

Terms defined in this glossary are in type that **looks like this** (bold type) on their first appearance on any two facing pages (a spread).

anaconda - the name of a group of large snakes that live in the hot and wet parts of South America

fierce - wild; ferocious

grasslands - an area of land with mostly grass and few trees; grassland can be hot and dry or wet and have more trees

talons - the claws of an animal, especially a bird of prey

termite - a small insect that lives in large colonies and eats the woody parts of plants and trees

Note to the Grown-Ups: Each "It's a Wildlife, Buddy!" book combines a whimsical narrative and factual background information to help children learn a little life lesson and a few things about some animals with which we share the world. We have the animal characters say and do things that are not possible for them in the wild to create stories that can appeal to children and that they can relate to. The stories can help children think about making friends, growing up, and other important parts of their lives. The fanciful stories are balanced by basic facts about the animals' lives and behaviors in nature. This combination creates a satisfying and informing reading experience whether an adult is reading to a child or a child is reading on his or her own.